FLAPPERS AND FAST WOMEN

A Book of Illustrations

Red Barn Kitchen Designs 2024

Introduction

The 1920s was a decade of enormous change, characterized by the rise of the automobile, changing roles of women, dramatic shifts in fashion, and the rapid evolution of both technology and social mores.

The early part of the decade saw the advent of the "flapper", young, daring, and fashionable, along with cinematic archetypes such as the vamp and the girl next door.

This book of illustrations is an attempt to catch some of that spirit. They are NOT historically accurate in any way shape or form, and should not be taken as a chronicle of 1920s' fashions.

The intent of these illustrations is strictly entertainment and decoration. This book is printed one sided, so pages can be removed if desired, without bleed through or having to choose between images.

We hope you enjoy them!

www.ingramcontent.com/pod-product-compliance
Lightning Source LLC
Chambersburg PA
CBHW040051240726
48664CB00004B/1144